Color Me
KITTENS

Color Me Kittens

13-Digit ISBN: 978-1-64643-415-2
10-Digit ISBN: 1-64643-415-3

This book may be ordered by mail from the publisher. Please include $5.99 for postage and handling. Please support your local bookseller first!

Books published by Cider Mill Press Book Publishers are available at special discounts for bulk purchases in the United States by corporations, institutions, and other organizations. For more information, please contact the publisher.

Cider Mill Press Book Publishers
"Where Good Books Are Ready for Press"
501 Nelson Place
Nashville, Tennessee 37214

cidermillpress.com

Typography: Epicursive Script, Filson Pro

Printed in the United States of America

23 24 25 26 27 VER 6 5 4 3

Color Me KITTENS

A Purr-fect Coloring Book

Illustrations by Yan Gu

CIDER MILL PRESS

BOOK PUBLISHERS

Introduction

Feeling stressed? Flop down with these purr-fect illustrations of cute, cuddly cats that will be sure to make you smile and help you relax. There is nothing quite like curling up and getting cozy with colors! These furry friends will leave you feline good and help your artistic side flourish.

Coloring is fun with friends, too! Grab your pawsome pals, snuggle up, and enjoy some cat-tastic conversation while creating beautiful memories. No matter how you are feeling, there is a cuddly kitten on the pages that follow sharing your mood, waiting to be brought to life. Improve your cat-titude with coloring and hang up your masterpieces once you are done! With kittens playing and sleeping in these meow-nificant designs, *Color Me Kittens* has something for all cat lovers!

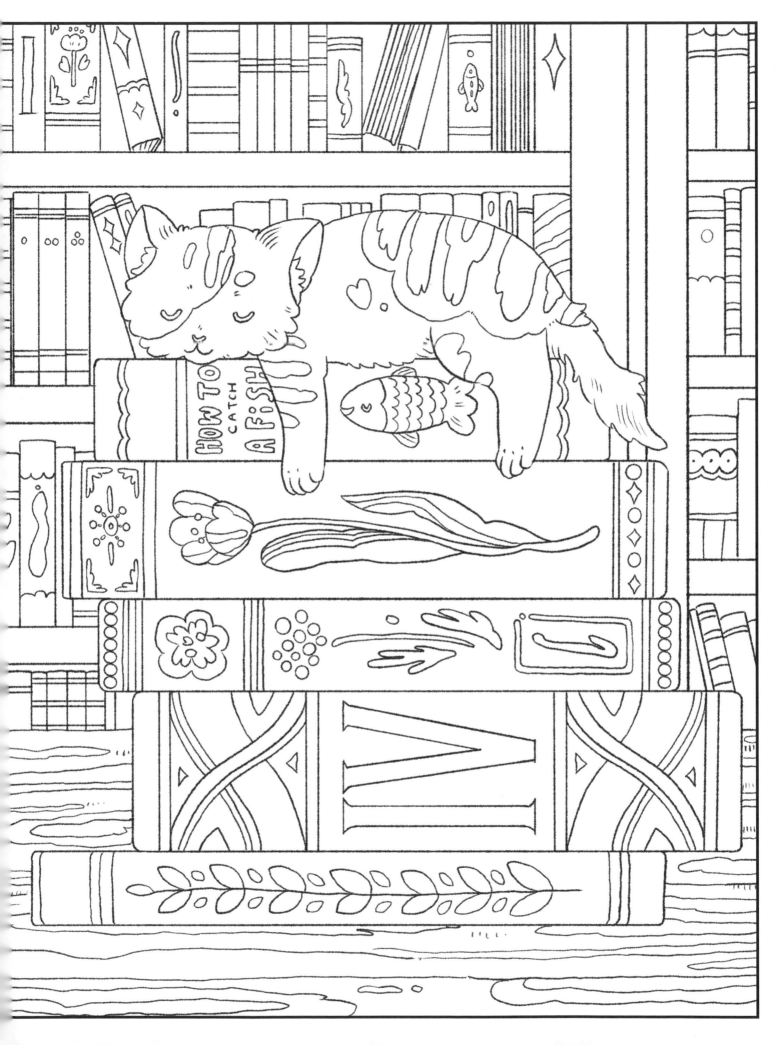

Share Your
MASTERPIECES

Don't keep your colorful creations to yourself—take a pic and share it on social media with the hashtag **#colormekittens** and tag us @cidermillpress!

#COLORMEKITTENS #COLORMEKITTENS
#COLORMEKITTENS #COLORMEKITTENS
#COLORMEKITTENS #COLORMEKITTENS
#COLORMEKITTENS #COLORMEKITTENS
#COLORMEKITTENS #COLORMEKITTENS
#COLORMEKITTENS #COLORMEKITTENS
#COLORMEKITTENS #COLORMEKITTENS
#COLORMEKITTENS #COLORMEKITTENS
#COLORMEKITTENS #COLORMEKITTENS
#COLORMEKITTENS #COLORMEKITTENS
#COLORMEKITTENS #COLORMEKITTENS
#COLORMEKITTENS #COLORMEKITTENS
#COLORMEKITTENS #COLORMEKITTENS
#COLORMEKITTENS #COLORMEKITTENS
#COLORMEKITTENS #COLORMEKITTENS
#COLORMEKITTENS #COLORMEKITTENS
#COLORMEKITTENS #COLORMEKITTENS
#COLORMEKITTENS #COLORMEKITTENS
#COLORMEKITTENS #COLORMEKITTENS
#COLORMEKITTENS #COLORMEKITTENS
#COLORMEKITTENS #COLORMEKITTENS

#COLORMEKITTENS #COLORMEKITTENS
#COLORMEKITTENS #COLORMEKITTENS
#COLORMEKITTENS #COLORMEKITTENS
#COLORMEKITTENS #COLORMEKITTENS
#COLORMEKITTENS #COLORMEKITTENS
#COLORMEKITTENS #COLORMEKITTENS
#COLORMEKITTENS #COLORMEKITTENS
#COLORMEKITTENS #COLORMEKITTENS
#COLORMEKITTENS #COLORMEKITTENS
#COLORMEKITTENS #COLORMEKITTENS
#COLORMEKITTENS #COLORMEKITTENS
#COLORMEKITTENS #COLORMEKITTENS
#COLORMEKITTENS #COLORMEKITTENS
#COLORMEKITTENS #COLORMEKITTENS
#COLORMEKITTENS #COLORMEKITTENS
#COLORMEKITTENS #COLORMEKITTENS
#COLORMEKITTENS #COLORMEKITTENS
#COLORMEKITTENS #COLORMEKITTENS
#COLORMEKITTENS #COLORMEKITTENS
#COLORMEKITTENS #COLORMEKITTENS
#COLORMEKITTENS #COLORMEKITTENS
#COLORMEKITTENS #COLORMEKITTENS

#COLORMEKITTENS #COLORMEKITTENS
#COLORMEKITTENS #COLORMEKITTENS
#COLORMEKITTENS #COLORMEKITTENS
#COLORMEKITTENS #COLORMEKITTENS
#COLORMEKITTENS #COLORMEKITTENS
#COLORMEKITTENS #COLORMEKITTENS
#COLORMEKITTENS #COLORMEKITTENS
#COLORMEKITTENS #COLORMEKITTENS
#COLORMEKITTENS #COLORMEKITTENS
#COLORMEKITTENS #COLORMEKITTENS
#COLORMEKITTENS #COLORMEKITTENS
#COLORMEKITTENS #COLORMEKITTENS
#COLORMEKITTENS #COLORMEKITTENS
#COLORMEKITTENS #COLORMEKITTENS
#COLORMEKITTENS #COLORMEKITTENS
#COLORMEKITTENS #COLORMEKITTENS
#COLORMEKITTENS #COLORMEKITTENS
#COLORMEKITTENS #COLORMEKITTENS
#COLORMEKITTENS #COLORMEKITTENS
#COLORMEKITTENS #COLORMEKITTENS
#COLORMEKITTENS #COLORMEKITTENS
#COLORMEKITTENS #COLORMEKITTENS

#COLORMEKITTENS #COLORMEKITTENS
#COLORMEKITTENS #COLORMEKITTENS
#COLORMEKITTENS #COLORMEKITTENS
#COLORMEKITTENS #COLORMEKITTENS
#COLORMEKITTENS #COLORMEKITTENS
#COLORMEKITTENS #COLORMEKITTENS
#COLORMEKITTENS #COLORMEKITTENS
#COLORMEKITTENS #COLORMEKITTENS
#COLORMEKITTENS #COLORMEKITTENS
#COLORMEKITTENS #COLORMEKITTENS
#COLORMEKITTENS #COLORMEKITTENS
#COLORMEKITTENS #COLORMEKITTENS
#COLORMEKITTENS #COLORMEKITTENS
#COLORMEKITTENS #COLORMEKITTENS
#COLORMEKITTENS #COLORMEKITTENS
#COLORMEKITTENS #COLORMEKITTENS
#COLORMEKITTENS #COLORMEKITTENS
#COLORMEKITTENS #COLORMEKITTENS
#COLORMEKITTENS #COLORMEKITTENS
#COLORMEKITTENS #COLORMEKITTENS
#COLORMEKITTENS #COLORMEKITTENS
#COLORMEKITTENS #COLORMEKITTENS
#COLORMEKITTENS #COLORMEKITTENS

About
CIDER MILL PRESS
BOOK PUBLISHERS

Good ideas ripen with time. From seed to harvest,
Cider Mill Press brings fine reading, information, and
entertainment together between the covers of its creatively
crafted books. Our Cider Mill bears fruit twice a year,
publishing a new crop of titles each spring and fall.

"Where Good Books Are Ready for Press"

501 Nelson Place
Nashville, Tennessee 37214

cidermillpress.com